YOUR KNOWLEDGE HAS VALUE

- We will publish your bachelor's and master's thesis, essays and papers

- Your own eBook and book - sold worldwide in all relevant shops

- Earn money with each sale

Upload your text at www.GRIN.com
and publish for free

Bibliographic information published by the German National Library:

The German National Library lists this publication in the National Bibliography; detailed bibliographic data are available on the Internet at http://dnb.dnb.de .

This book is copyright material and must not be copied, reproduced, transferred, distributed, leased, licensed or publicly performed or used in any way except as specifically permitted in writing by the publishers, as allowed under the terms and conditions under which it was purchased or as strictly permitted by applicable copyright law. Any unauthorized distribution or use of this text may be a direct infringement of the author s and publisher s rights and those responsible may be liable in law accordingly.

Imprint:

Copyright © 2018 GRIN Verlag
Print and binding: Books on Demand GmbH, Norderstedt Germany
ISBN: 9783668737525

This book at GRIN:

https://www.grin.com/document/430926

Mutinda Jackson

Using Registration for the Implementation of Projects

Monitoring and Evaluation

GRIN Verlag

GRIN - Your knowledge has value

Since its foundation in 1998, GRIN has specialized in publishing academic texts by students, college teachers and other academics as e-book and printed book. The website www.grin.com is an ideal platform for presenting term papers, final papers, scientific essays, dissertations and specialist books.

Visit us on the internet:

http://www.grin.com/

http://www.facebook.com/grincom

http://www.twitter.com/grin_com

REGISTRATION

Registration is the deposition of information on a **Register** that can be used for implementation of projects that need obtaining of accurate data about size, type, colour, mass, and other quantitative variables used. Registration will enable close monitoring of activities and ensure compliance with the rules and set of laws. Registration is a useful method in designing and implementing statistical projects. The data collected must be reliable, complete and timely to provide solution to the problem in evaluation.

In registration method, there are various types of data. Data on size, type, origin, capacity, is important in transportation registers. The processing of raw materials, processing capacity and sources of these materials are important for the monitoring and evaluation of the processing firm. Registers should capture new records and be able to indicate inactive records. For instance, licences must be renewed yearly. The data on licensing is useful since the records are updated annually (Council, 2015).

Registers are complex data collecting instrument. They require administrative procedures with effective data communications, storage and processing.

QUESTIONNAIRES

Questionnaires are subject forms filled in by respondents as provision of answers to the questions posed. Questionnaires can be adopted for a population or a sample segment. They collect both regular routine data and infrequent schedule data. The information obtained from questionnaires basically is about demographic features, practices of stakeholders and information about the respondents.

Questionnaire method requires respondents to fill out the forms. This requires a high level of literacy. Questionnaires are usually prepared using the major languages of the target group. Translation of languages must ensure accuracy in collection of the data. Questionnaires should be designed to be as simple and clear as possible, with sections and questions targeting the data needed. They can contain either prepared questions with blanks to be filled by the respondents, multiple-choice questions and open-ended questions.

INTERVIEW

Information from interviews is obtained through conversations between interviewer and the interviewee and recorded. Controlled interviews are performed using survey forms. However, in open interviews notes are taken while talking with respondents. These interpretations are then analysed. Interview data should be interpreted and analysed during and after interview by well trained enumerators. Pilot test forms designed for the interview are important in preparing the questionnaire. **Open-ended interviews** involve data-gathering research methods. Focus groups (5-15 individuals) compose of a cluster of enumerators whose beliefs, practices and opinions are in research. Panel survey involves the random selection of individuals from a group who agree to be available over an extended period. This is a stratified random sample from which data is elicited on a variety of issues.

On the other hand, **structured interviews** are conducted with a well-designed interview forms. The forms are filled by researchers instead of respondents, and in that, it differs from questionnaires. It is an expensive approach, more complicated questions asked. Data is validated as it is collected thereby improving data quality.

When Interviews are combined with observation method, enumerators verify the data collected from interviews through physical observations. An interview approach is used where a predetermined sub-set of an interview group is selected. With most variability experienced in time rather than space, the extra information about time increases significance results therefore better estimates analysed.

OBSERVATIONS

Observers make direct measurements on variables at the research site. These variables include temperature, length, weight and age. Observers make direct observations, conduct interviews, and survey using questionnaires. Adequate training and supervision is essential because the tasks are difficult. Decisions are made on the nature and extend of data collected. Observers therefore do not perform tasks on law enforcement, licensing and tax collection.

Inspectors are involved in law enforcement and surveillance playing important roles in verification. Reports are physically compared with observations. For instance, random samples verify their contents (product types, sizes, and grades), against container identification details. Inspection data is treated with caution because of sampling biasness. The potential bias of data by law-enforcement officers should be considered in the analyses.

Scientific study is usually carried out with the objective of obtaining observations on biological, environmental and chemical variables. The research is carried out at regular intervals to attain time sequential data. Key informants with specialised knowledge include academic specialists and community leaders. They are usually able to give an in-depth descriptive data. Participant-observation is a technique where the researcher spends an extended period of time living with a target group, observing their behaviour and participating in their practices. This is a good method of learning about the actual processes of decision-making (Huber et al, 2015).

Data logging is positioning and conveying of data on operations that involve location, speediness, title and use in the course of electronic instruments like timers, speedometers and GPS locators. Reporting in the systems databases and reports that aggregate data or remove identifiers will be relatively simple in comparing isolated spots against the confirmed site.

REPORTING

Enumerators do not directly undertake data collection in most complete enumeration approaches. They utilize external information basis. The sources are data forms filled by diverse professionals drawn in the exercise. Ordinary assent of necessary facts is part of professionals like doctors, teachers, market operators, and even customers. Records submitted by corporations are declarations and logbooks which enclose comprehensive information on definite property operations with nature and length of operations (Huber et al, 2015).

The benefit of using information is that facts are compiled by agents and occasionally availed in pre-processed plan. Discretion of information is a subject matter in the concurrence for data compliance and current numerical outputs. In **harvesting** job, essential data is required. The data collected could be inaccurate and thus validation from supervisors is required. During **post-harvesting** operations, data is used to get hold of information on markets, overheads and income, quantities and price intelligence of the produce.

Marketplace operation paperwork outlines a practical way of collecting statistics. Invoices and sales slips are considered for comfortable approach and accessibility to make certain totality of reporting. Trade data is information from customs and other allied sources on trade used in socio-economic indicators. Imports / exports information available, mainly duty and incentive figures have restricted utility in estimating the entire making except means to establish the percentage for local creation and utilization.

In managing a project's data quality, we develop a data quality plan. Data Quality Plan has six components that are:

Definition of a Record: Rationale of understanding the entire set of data rudiments necessary to congregate the wants. Records definitions may be diverse depending on the sort of the program. List of the data essentials are likely to be composed.

Timeliness: Justification on the duration of time involving data gathering and entry force the accuracy of the information entered and openness once required. Features are recognized by program type, screening the expectations for the span of time connecting collection and entry of data. The exception is that the project may possibly want to implement different timelines for dissimilar programs.

Completeness: underlying principle is that incompleteness make client care, package delivery, analyse data and report validity. These factors involve a manuscript, by program technique, for the completeness of facts module sets that all clients' services are utilized. Exceptions arising comprise "Don't identify", "unidentified" and "Rejected". Standard is likely to be altered for different program types or subpopulations.

Accuracy: in rationalising, information must reflect what is presented by client. The facts are understood, collected, and precisely recorded. Data substantiation practices, steadiness in data gathering forms, habitual preparation on data basics and definitions, implements that accomplish a universal understanding of fundamentals and responses are exceptions of precision as a constituent of this plan.

Monitoring ensures that the standards are being met. Document expectation for monitoring activities and the methods that data quality is monitored are factors involved. The exceptions are that it is not a monitoring plan; it outlines the general guidelines and sets forth expectations and tasks in general terms.

Incentives and Enforcement: the rationale is reinforcing the importance of quality data through incentives and enforcements. A list and description of incentive and enforcement measures for compliance are factored in. The exceptions include public recognition and progress, bonus points on local scoring of funds applications and funding impacts for non-compliance.

Dissemination of information in a project refers to the process of making results and deliverables of a project available to the stakeholders and to the wider audience. Dissemination is essential for take-up, and take-up is crucial for the success of the project.

There are a broad variety of dissemination ways. It is important therefore to select the ones to get your message to the target audience and achieve the purpose.

Newsletters, flyers and press releases can be used as ways of creating awareness among the stakeholders in the project, both internal and external stakeholders. Reports, journal entries, and web sites can be used as ways of transmitting information about the project to different stakeholders. Conference presentations and web sites are ways used to promote the project and the outcomes experienced by stakeholders.

Moreover, traditional dissemination ways can be useful than typical strategies. For instance, workshops or online discussions yield high levels of engagement from stakeholders. This is relevant when there is conflict or resistance to a certain type of information.

Face-to-face communication is suitable for group or individual meetings and can be either formal or informal. It allows for instant feedback, and you are better able to gauge whether the others understand what is being communicated. One disadvantage is that meetings can be costly if participants have to be brought in from other states and/or countries. In addition, you need time and resources to facilitate such meetings, with staff dedicated to ensuring the agenda is followed, the meeting starts and ends on time, and minutes are taken and distributed to all participants.

During this age of information with access to the internet, mobile devices and computers, project information can be distributed in electronic version form. Given the shortage of time and tight budget controls for some projects, communication via the Internet is faster, cheaper and easier to retain for record purposes. Email works best for brief updates on project status, while large files can be sent as attachments or stored in the cloud. You can also maintain a project portal or intranet site to share project data. A major disadvantage is the risk of data loss or unauthorized access to confidential project information by hackers.

Hard-copy communications including letters, memoranda and reports are used to disseminate information to various stakeholders. Due to their visual and textual characteristics, they can be edited and revised several times to shape them for maximum effect before being distributed. In addition, they provide a permanent record of the communication which can be archived for later retrieval. A major disadvantage is storage. They require paper, which can be cumbersome to file and store in large quantities. Aging of the documents and susceptibility to loss or damage can lead to difficulties in managing project records Mascia, et al, 2014).

In conferencing way of disseminating information, calls and even video calls are used to get large groups together. A telephone or online tool like Skype allow for real-time video collaboration with all the parties able to see each other. Video conferencing tools also provide white boards and other options for document sharing and editing. One disadvantage concerns time zones -- it can be difficult to get everyone scheduled in a session depending on where they are in the world. Another is that the personal aspect of a conversation is taken away, and conferencing etiquette may not be observed by some users such as being on time and paying attention.

The key features of monitoring and evaluation reports as presented to various stakeholders. First, M&E reports have outputs that reflect the critical stated strategic objectives of the organization. Secondly, these reports provide clear indicators against which the organization is working, and being measured; and that within the organization, information for the outputs being measured is available and verifiable. Thirdly, a good M&E reports identify key issues and root of the problems that are addressed to the stakeholders.

A Monitoring and Evaluation reports must be self oriented, cost effective and result oriented. They should be updated regularly and must track and with effect, support the policy reform process. These reports should be user friendly in understanding the current issues of the relevant policy. A rationale for how future performance targets are set is a feature of these reports. These reports should make the decision making at management levels easy and efficient.

M&E reports must have technically accurate information to convey to the stakeholders. This report should have information that is legal, ethical and due regard for the welfare of the stakeholders. An effective and good M&E report presents its findings in a positive way and as constructive criticism. These reports identify the responsible persons to finalize the actions agreed.

The approaches in Community Participatory Monitoring and Evaluation (PM&E) are more cost-effective, accurate and sustainable than the conventional approaches. Participation in decision-making processes can also motivate people to want to see those decisions implemented effectively Mascia, et al, 2014).

However, PM&E is not without its critics. Crucially, labelling M&E as 'participatory' does not necessarily guarantee that all stakeholder groups have participated, and there are often issues around who participates and who is excluded from these processes. Subsequently, the representativeness of the findings and recommendations of participatory evaluations have been criticised. PM&E encompasses a wide range of approaches that include values such as shared learning, democratic processes, joint decision making, co-ownership, mutual respect and empowerment. Participatory Rural Appraisal (PRA) encompasses a broad range of methods to enable local people to analyse their own realities as the basis for planning, monitoring and evaluating development activities. PRA uses group exercises to facilitate information sharing, analysis, and action among stakeholders.

Beneficiary feedback systems seek to collect key stakeholders' views about the quality and impact of a development agency's work. This approach has grown in popularity and has been supported by a range of donors. While beneficiary feedback systems are likely to improve sustainability and can empower beneficiaries, they may present only a partial impression of beneficiaries' views, and there has been a lack of rigorous evaluation of their impact.

Key informant interviews are a rapid assessment methodology that can be used as an intermediate indicator of outcomes as an alternative or supplement to full impact assessments.

The Most Significant Change (MSC) technique involves the collection of change stories from the field level, and the systematic selection of the most significant of these. These selected stories are then discussed and critically reflected on to help determine the impact of the development programme or activity (Tsui, et al, 2014).

Outcome Mapping (OM) is an alternative to theory-based approaches to evaluation that rely on a cause–effect framework. It recognises that multiple, non-linear events lead to change. It focuses on people and changes of behaviour and how far development interventions have built the capacity of the local community. Outcome mapping assumes only that a contribution has been made, and never attempts attribution. OM is well-suited to areas involving complex change processes, capacity building work, and knowledge and decision-making processes. Shifting to OM's learning-oriented mode requires donors to adopt more realistic expectations and to dispense with the idea of 'controlling' change processes. Crucially, OM must be underpinned by real trust between the donor, project implementers and partners.

References

Council, M. S. (2015). Monitoring and evaluation.

Heller, D., Hubert, W., Lutz, S., Maule, A., Naiman, R., Ruggerone, G., ... & Wood, C. (2015). Review of the Monitoring and Evaluation Plan for the Walla Walla Spring Chinook Hatchery Master Plan (public review draft): Response Requested.

Huber, J., Nepal, S., Bauer, D., Wessels, I., Fischer, M. R., & Kiessling, C. (2015). Tools and instruments for needs assessment, monitoring and evaluation of health research capacity development activities at the individual and organizational level: a systematic review. Health research policy and systems, 13(1), 80.

Mascia, M. B., Pailler, S., Thieme, M. L., Rowe, A., Bottrill, M. C., Danielsen, F., ... & Burgess, N. D. (2014). Commonalities and complementarities among approaches to conservation monitoring and evaluation. Biological Conservation, 169, 258-267.

Tsui, J., Hearn, S., & Young, J. (2014). Monitoring and evaluation of policy influence and advocacy. London: ODI Working paper, 395.

YOUR KNOWLEDGE HAS VALUE

- We will publish your bachelor's and master's thesis, essays and papers

- Your own eBook and book - sold worldwide in all relevant shops

- Earn money with each sale

Upload your text at www.GRIN.com
and publish for free